What you should know about DRUGS

What you should know about

Dr. Charles W. Gorodetzky
and Dr. Samuel T. Christian

HARCOURT BRACE JOVANOVICH, INC. · New York

Curriculum-Related Books are relevant
to current interests of young people
and to topics in the school curriculum.

Contents

32972

The authors wish to thank the staff of Phoenix House for their invaluable help and cooperation, and most especially for allowing them to interview several children at one treatment center in New York. Brief anonymous passages based on these and other interviews appear throughout the book.

Foreword

In the past ten years, abuse of an ever-expanding number of drugs has increased markedly in the United States and other Western countries. The problem has broken the bounds of the economically and socially deprived areas of the large cities and is spreading into the more affluent suburbs. Increasing numbers of college students are experimenting with drugs. Some are becoming dependent on them and dropping out of education and out of the mainstream of society. Even more frightening is the spread of drug abuse into the high schools and even into the elementary schools. All sorts of people—legislators, physicians, ministers, teachers, parents—are deeply concerned. Despite a large variety of experimental and preventive programs inaugurated by the federal government, the states, and the cities, the problem continues to grow.

It is natural to turn to education as the cornerstone of preventive programs. But what kind of education? Where can teachers find the proper sort of educational material? At what point in the educational process should information about drugs be first taught? Most states have requirements that information about tobacco, alcohol, and drugs be introduced in the upper elementary grades, but the material available is frequently inaccurate, misleading, and out of date. Better material is available at the high-school and college levels, but is too advanced for elementary-school children. Since drug abuse is now involving elementary-school children in some localities, it is urgent that information appropriate for the upper elementary grades be available.

This book meets that unfilled need. The authors are both researchers in the field of drug abuse. The content of the book is factual. It tells it "like it is." The well-established facts about the dangers and damage of various kinds of drug abuse are recounted unemotionally and without moralizing. The good things about drugs, when properly used under medical supervision, are also covered.

The book is designed for children in the upper elementary grades and is written in language that children in that age group can understand. The book is an outgrowth of the authors' experience in teaching (as volunteers) facts about drugs to youngsters in elementary schools in their home town of Lexington, Kentucky.

The book will also be as useful to parents and teachers, who have need of accurate information about drugs, as it is to the children.

HARRIS ISBELL, M.D.
Professor of Medicine and Pharmacology,
    University of Kentucky College of Medicine

Member, Panel of Experts on Drug Dependence,
    World Health Organization

Member, Committee on Problems of Drug Dependence,
    National Research Council, National Academy
    of Sciences

Headache? take aspirin / Tension? take
Compōz

when you're under
occasional stress,
helps you
Work relaxed
Relax to sleep
Sedative for temporary relief
of simple nervous tension
Compōz

CONTAC
CONTINUOUS ACTION DECONGESTANT CAPSULES

Alka-Selt

GELUSIL
100 TAB

GELUSIL
ANTACID
TABLETS

Nite-Rest

VICKS
FORMULA
4
COUGH
SAFE/FAST ACTING
Dōz
ALERT TABLETS

EX-LAX

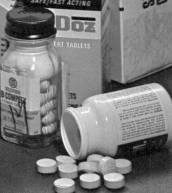
B COMPLEX

Drugs Are All Around Us

What is a drug?

Sugar is a drug; so is salt. Penicillin is also a drug. The nicotine in cigarettes is a drug. Alcohol is a drug. And of course heroin, marijuana, diet pills, glue, and all the other substances that are causing problems for so many young people today are drugs.

What do all drugs have in common? They all produce a change in us. A *drug** is any substance that

---

* All words printed in italics are listed, with definitions, in the Glossary for convenient reference.

Almost everyone is familiar
with some commonly used drugs.

affects living matter. The change produced by a drug is called a *drug effect*. In general, the greater the amount taken, the greater the drug effect.

Many drugs are known as *medicines*. These are the drugs given by doctors to cure the diseases we get and to ease the discomfort sickness causes. For example, if you have a cold you might be given a drug called aspirin. Aspirin has the effect of lowering fever and, therefore, helps in relieving the discomfort caused by the cold. In the case of a severe infection a drug called an *antibiotic* may be given. This drug kills the germs causing the infection and helps you get better faster.

Other medicines ease pain. Aspirin is used by many people for minor pains such as headaches. Most people keep a supply of it in their medicine cabinets.

But no drug is always harmless. For example: Everyone requires a certain amount of sugar to maintain good health. But too much sugar can produce bad effects, such as overweight. And while an aspirin can harmlessly make a headache go away, a small handful can cause severe illness. A bottleful, swallowed in a few gulps, can kill. The fact is that any drug—any substance we put into our bodies—can be dangerous.

Some drugs are produced naturally—in plants, for instance—and are collected and refined by man

It has become nearly impossible to pick up a popular magazine or turn on a TV set without seeing advertisements for drugs.

for his use. Others are made in laboratories by combining simple chemicals.

There are many ways to take drugs into the body. The most common are by mouth and by injection. The time necessary for a drug to take effect and the length of time the effects last will depend both on the amount of drug and the way it is put into the body. A large amount of drug will usually produce its effects sooner—and the effects will last longer—than a small amount. A drug taken by needle will show its effects quickly (sometimes within a few seconds), while a drug that is swallowed may not produce effects for a half hour or longer.

Naming a drug

The same drug is often referred to by many names. Sometimes the actual chemical name of the substance is used, but chemical names are often long and complicated, so each drug is also assigned a "common name." The common name is also called the *generic name.* More than one drug company can manufacture any one drug, and each company may assign its own name to the drug. This name is called a *trade name,* and it is spelled with a capital letter. For example, a common sleeping pill has the complex chemical name 5-phenyl-5-ethyl malonyl urea. Its generic name is phenobarbital, and it is sold by one drug company under the trade name Luminal.

This book will generally refer to all drugs by their generic names, though a number of the better-known trade names will also be mentioned.

Why do we need to know about drugs?

When used properly to treat illness, medicines are a great benefit to mankind. However, when a medicine is taken for any reason except as a treatment for sickness, it is being abused. Also, drugs for which no medical use has been found are sometimes abused. Such *drug abuse* often leads to harm to the individual and to society.

Many young people find out about drugs through friends and classmates in high school, junior high, or even in elementary school. Unfortunately, while these people will talk about how the drugs bring joy and about how they "expand" the mind, they often ignore facts about the tragic effects the abuse of drugs can have: the sickness and pain, the need to steal to pay for drugs after the mind and body have come to depend upon them, the possibility of arrest and imprisonment. As one young girl who had abused drugs said, "Most of the people who are dealing to you tell you that you get a groovy feeling— and this, that, and the other thing—but they don't say anything about the actual bad effects."

Why do people abuse drugs?

Most people, even youngsters, know something of the dangers of abusing drugs. If that is so, why do they begin taking them? For some, it is a way of escaping from an unhappy world. Drugs "served the purpose of blurring certain ugly realities of ghetto experience," said one boy who found himself surrounded by hopelessness and failure. "It helped my nose not to smell the urine-soaked hallways. I didn't feel the garbage underfoot, I didn't hear the police sirens tearing through the black jungle." The boy was only thirteen years old when he spoke—he had been introduced to drugs at an even earlier age.

The world in which this young boy lived was far more unpleasant than most people's. Yet many children who are better off find themselves tempted by drugs. One boy who comes from an upper-middle-class family put it this way: "Most of the kids who were using drugs really just wanted to escape from the pressures of school, of trying to find something, some goals and things like that, and most of us were really the same. We didn't really care or have anything that we were really there for."

For some it is curiosity, the desire to find out what it is like. "The main reason I started taking drugs is, I had a lot of curiosity about, you know, what's this thing that everybody's talking about?

10

Some young people think that drugs will provide
an escape from their surroundings.

Drugs. You know—pot." Many people who begin abusing drugs for this reason believe they will try it once or twice, then stop. However, this is often not what happens.

Still other youngsters are caught by their inability to say "no" to friends. "A lot of my friends were trying drugs. I felt left out. I wanted very much to be part of the crowd. I just wanted to feel I belonged to something, you know. I saw this big thing going on and it gave me an opportunity. I felt like I would be, you know, like an outcast if I didn't. Like everybody else is doing it, so why shouldn't I? I didn't want to be square."

Others use drugs to defy their parents. "I started because of the restrictions my parents had on me. I wanted to do my own thing."

Yet another reason sometimes given is that of mind-expansion. "I had heard that some drugs would give me more insight and understanding—that they would make me a better person."

What problems result from drug abuse?

People who abuse drugs often find themselves in serious trouble. Because of the effects of some drugs, the user may cause himself physical harm. He may change or even lose his ability to think straight. His behavior and entire pattern of living may be altered.

12

A friend offering drugs can put you on the spot.

He may drop out of school, lose his job, or be unable to participate in the life of his family and friends. He may steal in order to get money to buy drugs. He may even wind up in jail.

What help is available to the drug abuser?

Many people who start abusing drugs find it difficult to stop without help. For these people, help is available. The federal and state governments and many communities have programs to aid those who want to stop using drugs. But even with the help of doctors and other specialists, quitting is not easy. Clearly, it is better by far not to begin using drugs.

One fifteen-year-old boy put it this way. "I wish I'd never started using drugs. This whole thing, you know, it's been like a nightmare. When I finish this treatment program, I think I can stay away from drugs. I want to go back to school. I feel like I've wasted three years of my life."

The drug abuser and the law

The use of drugs for treating disease is carefully regulated by laws. Drug companies must have a license to make them, druggists must be licensed to sell them, and only doctors may prescribe them. Anyone who manufactures or sells drugs without a license, or who has them in his possession without a doctor's prescription, is breaking the law. The punishments for breaking these laws are stiff; they may include both a fine and a jail term. A person who is convicted under these laws then has a "police record," which may make it difficult to get a job, or even a driver's license, for the rest of his life.

2 Narcotics

Narcotics are one of the oldest and most useful types of drugs that doctors have. *Opium* is a narcotic. Drugs that are made from opium and drugs that have effects like those of opium are also called narcotics. Opium itself is a mixture of drugs that come from the opium poppy, a flower that grows wild in Asia Minor, and is grown on farms in India, China, Egypt, and Turkey. Two of the drugs in opium are the pain-killers *morphine* and *codeine*. Other narcotics can be made from these two drugs. *Heroin* is one of them.

Some other narcotics can be made without using the opium poppy at all. For instance two other pain-killing drugs, *meperidine (Demerol)* and *methadone (Dolophine),* are made in the laboratory from simple chemicals.

Medical uses

Doctors give narcotics mainly to kill pain. They are the best drugs known for this purpose, strong enough to relieve even the terrible pain of heart attacks and certain types of cancer. Surgeons use them to relieve the pain patients feel after an operation, and dentists use them to relieve severe toothaches.

Surgeons also give narcotics to calm patients before operations, since they are often scared about what is going to happen to them. One of the narcotics, codeine, helps to stop coughing, so small amounts of it are included in some cough medicines. Narcotics also help people with diarrhea. Doctors often prescribe a medicine called *paregoric,* which contains opium, for this purpose.

Effects

When a person takes a narcotic, the drug produces certain effects on his body and mind. It causes his breathing to become slow. Very large doses can kill a person by stopping his breathing altogether. Narcotics can also make people feel sick to their stomachs and cause them to vomit. They can cause constipation and make the skin feel itchy. Narcotics also affect the small black center of the eye, called the pupil—they make the pupil get very small. Often it is possible to tell if a person has taken a narcotic by looking at his eyes.

Probably the narcotic that is abused most is heroin. It is made from morphine and is not prescribed by doctors in this country at all. People who use it must buy it illegally from *pushers*. Users call it *horse, H, smack,* and other names.

Characteristics of abuse

How do people use heroin? What effects are they seeking? At the beginning they may just sniff in the white powder, but soon they dissolve it in water and inject it. At first they inject it under the skin, then progress to shooting it directly into a vein. The user calls this process *mainlining*. He feels the effects of the drug much more strongly and quickly this way.

Following this kind of shot, the user experiences a warm and intensely pleasant feeling. This is referred to as a *rush,* and lasts at most for a few minutes. One boy who used to use heroin explained what happened when he gave himself a shot of the drug: "You get this kind of warm feeling all over, and then you feel very inactive to the point where you can

"You can hardly hold your head up, and you're very tired."

hardly hold your head up, you know, to keep it from dropping down, and you're very tired." The heroin user likes to just sit around alone in a kind of light sleep called *coasting*. His head droops, or nods. Another user explained, "It's a feeling of really not feeling. You are blocking out reality. It's like a feeling of being relieved from your problems."

It makes most people calm. Many people imagine heroin users as "dope fiends" who want to fight and attack people. But in fact the drug has just the opposite effect on the people who use it.

Because it usually gives the user a pleasant feeling, he may try it again and again. If he uses it often, the dose he has been taking does not keep on giving him the same feeling. His body is said to have become "tolerant" to the drug, so he has to take bigger and bigger doses to get the same effect.

In some ways this *tolerance* to a drug is similar to what happens when you jump into cold water. At first your body feels icy, but then it becomes used to the water and it no longer feels cold. Your body has become tolerant to the cold water. You would have to jump into even colder water to feel as cold as you did at first.

If someone keeps on taking heroin, he may come to need fifty times as much as his first dose to produce the same feeling. Many drugs besides heroin and other narcotics also produce tolerance.

If a user keeps taking larger and larger amounts of heroin, he finds that something else happens. When he tries to stop taking the drug, he gets terribly sick. His body has developed an actual need for the drug. This need is called *physical dependence*. His body has become so used to the drug that it needs it constantly —no longer just to produce the original effect but to avoid the sickness.

It takes only a few weeks for a user's body to build up physical dependence on narcotics. When he stops taking the drug now, he starts getting sick in about twelve hours. He shakes with chills and has sweats and fever. Goose bumps rise on his skin, his eyes and nose run, he gets sick to his stomach and may vomit. His stomach hurts and he has diarrhea. He cannot even go to sleep, because he is restless and his muscles keep twitching and hurting.

This sickness is called *withdrawal illness*. Although it makes the victim suffer, it seldom kills him. The severe part of the sickness lasts about two weeks, but it is months before the user is back to normal. In fact, he may never be completely normal again.

The physical dependence that causes withdrawal illness develops very quickly. The more drug the user takes and the more often he takes it, the more severe his illness will be when he stops.

One young boy, who had used heroin for two years, described the effects of withdrawal as follows:

The pain and misery brought on by withdrawal illness can make the victim feel sicker than he has ever felt before.

"I had terrible diarrhea. I felt like I had pneumonia and bronchitis all at the same time. And with the diarrhea I couldn't stop going to the bathroom. It got so bad that I couldn't even get up to go to the bathroom. My knees were weak and my bones hurt. My stomach had cramps. It was so bad that it's hard to describe. I felt like I was going to die."

Not only does a heroin user's body develop a need for the drug, but so does his mind. He develops an emotional need for the drug effect to help him forget about his problems. This need is called *psychological dependence,* and it can create such a strong habit that the user feels he cannot face life without the drug. You probably know children who cannot sleep unless they have a light on in their room. They have a psychological dependence on the light, although this is not a dangerous dependence. A user's need for heroin is the same sort of thing, but it is much much stronger.

People who develop dependence on drugs are called *drug addicts.* A person dependent on heroin is a *heroin addict.* He shows tolerance to the drug as well as physical and psychological dependence on it. This condition is sometimes referred to as being *"strung out."*

The life of an addict is almost always terrible. He is completely controlled by the drug. Once a person has become addicted to a narcotic, his need

for it, both physical and psychological, becomes so great that he spends his entire energy, all of his time, and all of his money trying to get enough drugs to satisfy his habit. Since it is against the law to buy narcotics without a prescription, this is not easy.

Here is how a high-school student named Jimmy described what his life was like when he was a heroin addict. "I gave up all pretenses of being a student, of being anything in life. I just felt like I was doomed to be an addict the rest of my life. I was spending about $50 or $60 a day to satisfy my habit. I was dealing drugs to get the money. In the beginning I was just dealing on a small scale and then eventually I began to deal heroin to all the kids in school—my friends, you know. I lost a lot of friends in that time. I was beating them, conning them out of money. You see, I didn't care any more about friendship. I didn't care anything about anything except the drug itself."

Since it is against the law for anyone, even licensed druggists, to sell heroin, the drug is handled almost entirely by criminals—people who usually don't care what they sell you as long as they get the money. They mix the heroin with other things—like powdered milk, sugar, or talcum powder—to make it go farther. This process is known as *cutting* the drug. Usually the drug has been cut several times by different dealers before it is finally sold to a user.

By this time, the user cannot know what he is

25

Illegal drugs change hands in a deserted doorway.

Sometimes an O.D. victim is lucky and gets medical attention before it is too late.

actually buying. Often there is so little heroin in the packet that an addict will have to buy a great deal to satisfy his habit. On the other hand, a dealer may sell him a portion that has not been cut as much as he is used to, so he runs the risk of accidentally taking an overdose, or an *"O.D."*

An overdose may make him very sick, and he may even die of it. In New York City alone hundreds of people die each year from overdose of narcotics.

Jimmy was lucky. He took an overdose once, but he managed to live through it. "It all happened pretty fast. First it was like I knew it was a beautiful shot. I mean when it hit, the rush was the strongest I ever had. And then the purple and black started coming in, and I went under—blacked out. That's all I remember. I remember, though, the fear of dying—but at that point, I tell you, like I wasn't even sure if I wanted to die or not."

Often the addict has to spend $75 or $100 a day. In order to get this kind of money, he frequently has to steal. One boy who had been taking heroin for two years explained, "In order to support the habit, I had to do a number of things that I didn't like to do, like stealing from my family. From my mother alone I must have stolen at least $400, and like even though she was my mother and she had raised me, it really didn't make any difference; my heroin habit came first.

"And I did other things, like stealing from old ladies, robbing cleaners, grocery stores, even selling drugs to other kids. It got to a point where I didn't care for anybody, family or not. Whenever my habit came down on me and I needed heroin, whichever way I could get the money, any way, that's the way I would get it."

Because he has to steal or sell drugs illegally in order to get enough money for his habit, the addict will usually spend much of his life in prison. The penalties for selling narcotics are severe.

Even if the addict is not arrested or "busted," he cannot always get enough money for the drugs he needs. Then he gets withdrawal illness.

In addition to the dangers of the drug itself, another problem is that the addict is often careless about the needles he uses for injecting the drug. Doctors, of course, sterilize a needle before giving an injection. But addicts are often beyond caring about such things, and in their haste to get a shot of the drug they will use any needle they can get hold of. Severe diseases can result from using dirty needles. A bad infection of the liver called hepatitis, a blood disease called malaria, bad sores on the skin, and infections of the heart valves are constant dangers to addicts who use dirty needles. Usually addicts die fifteen or twenty years sooner than other people.

Most addicts spend a good deal of time in jail.

3 Marijuana

Marijuana is a drug that, like opium, has been known for many centuries. It belongs to a class of drugs known as *hallucinogens*. A hallucinogen is a drug that affects the mind in such a way as to bring on *hallucinations*—a disorder of the senses that makes you see, or hear, or smell, or feel things that are not really there.

Sometimes a hallucination may seem normal. For example, you could think you see a friend walking down the street, looking just the way he always does, and even hear him speak to you in his usual voice—

A friend may look as if he had four faces.

but he would not really be there. However, hallucinations may also seem weird and distorted. You might think you see your friend and hear him talking—but he appears to have three heads, four arms, and five feet. And his voice sounds like chalk screeching on a blackboard.

Small amounts of hallucinogenic drugs do not produce effects like these. Low doses usually produce a slight distortion of the senses—a table may feel as if it had a coat of fur, or a whisper may sound like a shout. There is a table there, and someone is whispering—you simply perceive these things as different from the way they are. Larger amounts can make you see a table, with or without fur, when there is no table there at all.

Although this is a hallucination, the person who goes through it is usually aware that these strange experiences come because he has taken a drug. At very high doses, however, full hallucinations appear—the person may no longer remember that they are produced by the drug. He believes that what he is feeling is totally real. As you might imagine, this can be a terrifying experience, and a person may even feel he has lost his mind.

Marijuana comes from the Indian hemp plant, which grows in all mild climates including the United States. The plant contains a mixture of drugs. Marijuana is made from the flowering tops and leaves.

It can be prepared and taken in many ways. In the United States marijuana is usually prepared by breaking up the leaves and tops, and sometimes the stems, into a tobacco-like mixture. This is often called *hay, grass, weed,* or *pot.* The mixture is rolled into cigarettes and smoked. The frequently used slang names for marijuana cigarettes include *reefers, joints,* and *sticks.* The leaves may be used to make a drink sometimes referred to as *bhang.* The tops of the plant and the leaves may also be treated to make a strong mixture of active drugs. This is then made into a small brick often referred to as *hashish,* which is eaten or put into a pipe and smoked.

Medical uses

Over the years many attempts have been made to find uses for marijuana in treating sickness. Although there is no proven medical use for this mixture, it is still available as a medicine in some parts of the world. For the most part, however, drugs with more reliable and proven effects are almost always used.

Effects

The effects of marijuana are like those of small doses of any hallucinogen. Some people say that smoking

ABOVE: The marijuana plant.
BELOW LEFT: A marijuana cigarette being rolled.
BELOW RIGHT: A "joint" in a pack of regular cigarettes.

marijuana calms them and makes them feel good. They become happy and sometimes silly and talkative. After larger amounts, they report that it distorts the way they experience things. Colors look brighter and more vivid than usual. Walls look wavy or seem to be moving. Music sounds clearer. Time may appear to pass very slowly.

One boy described it this way. "Every sound seemed to have a feeling to it. It made my body feel like it was transparent. Like deep tones, especially bass tones, they made my bones feel like they were shaking. It felt like every fiber of my body could feel my clothes—like I was really aware of my skin and everything it came into contact with. Music had a different meaning to it, you know—it was like I could pick up on rhythms that I would normally just overlook. And it became like, you know, it was just groovy and it made me feel like laughing a lot. I used to crack up constantly. Every time I smoked pot I would just die laughing because stupid things made me laugh. I could forget about everything."

People often seek such effects in order to produce or heighten feelings of pleasure. If the user is very sensitive, or if the marijuana happens to contain a large amount of active drug, he may experience full hallucinations. Physical effects of marijuana include an increase in the rate of the heartbeat. Also the eyes get red and bloodshot.

Red eye—one of the immediate effects of smoking marijuana.

There may also possibly be effects of marijuana that occur only after long continuous use of the drug. However, at this time there is very little knowledge of the nature or seriousness of these effects or whether they occur at all. It has been very difficult to study the effects of marijuana scientifically because of the lack of knowledge of what the active drugs might be. In addition, the amount of active drug in any given batch of marijuana is usually unknown, and apparently the batches differ a great deal.

Methods of analyzing marijuana are now being developed. Also pure preparations of suspected active drugs from marijuana are becoming available for study by scientists. This should lead to increasing knowledge about the true effects of marijuana.

Characteristics of abuse

Marijuana probably does not produce tolerance in the body, and using it does not seem to lead to physical dependence. But most experts agree that marijuana can lead to psychological dependence. That is, some users come to feel they just cannot face life without the aid of the drug.

In this country marijuana is usually smoked in groups, often in a party setting. At such a *"pot party"* most smokers are familiar with the effects they are seeking, and expect them. In fact, what a smoker

feels depends greatly on what he expects to feel. This can also depend on what people tell him he should feel, and the kind of setting in which he uses the drug. At this stage of our knowledge we cannot be sure whether some of the reported effects are actually caused by the drug or just imagined by the user.

It has been estimated that in the United States as many as 12 million people have used marijuana at least once. Most of these are young people, probably under thirty years of age. It has become increasingly popular in colleges, high schools, and even in junior high schools and elementary schools. Sometime during your school career you are very likely to meet people using marijuana.

What are the hazards of marijuana? Someone who is sensitive or who uses a marijuana preparation containing a large amount of active drug may experience a severe distortion of his senses. He may even develop full hallucinations. However, such drastic reactions to marijuana are quite rare. It has also been claimed that marijuana use leads to crime and also to automobile accidents. There is little scientific evidence to support such claims, though one would certainly expect that it would be dangerous to drive a car while *"high"* on marijuana.

One young boy told this story: "My friends and I had been to a pot party in the city. We were all a little stoned, I guess, but I decided we had to go home anyway. I had my father's car, and we started back on the turnpike. It was a beautiful day without much traffic, and we were all grooving on the scenery whizzing by. I wasn't paying any attention to how fast we were going, but I was paying enough attention to see the flashing light in my mirror. I pulled over right away. We didn't want any trouble, now of all times. One of my friends threw the last joint out the window before we stopped. As soon as the cop walked up, I began apologizing for speeding. Who knew how fast we had been going? He looked at me kind of funny, and said, 'Buddy, you were going fifteen miles an hour.' "

Marijuana can lead to the use of stronger drugs, although it does not always do so. Most narcotic addicts began by smoking marijuana, but this is not the same as saying that all people who smoke marijuana go on to heroin. However, his experience with marijuana often increases the user's curiosity about the effects of other drugs. Smoking marijuana gets him into a drug-taking crowd and may get him accustomed to using drugs to run away from his problems. Probably those who have used marijuana are more likely to go on to other drugs than those who have never used any drugs at all. In addition, some people can become heavy marijuana users, often called *"pot-heads."* They usually drop out of society

Some find out the hard way the penalties for breaking the law.

and become totally involved with taking all kinds of drugs as a way of life.

The use of marijuana is against the law. Having marijuana in your possession, giving it to someone, or selling it is a serious crime. Penalties may in some cases be as severe as for violations involving narcotics, and may lead to a police record for a *felony*.

Although there are some people who feel that the laws should be changed, the use of marijuana remains illegal. You should be aware of the possible penalties in your community for breaking the law.

4 LSD and Other Hallucinogens

In April 1943 a Swiss scientist named Albert Hofmann was studying drugs made from chemicals found in the ergot fungus. This fungus grows on the common grains rye and wheat. While working with one of these drugs one day in the laboratory, he began to feel strange. He got dizzy and restless. The shape of people and objects around him looked different. He couldn't concentrate. He felt as if he were in a dream.

Unable to continue his work, he went home and lay down. When he closed his eyes, he saw fantastic pictures, vivid in color, with objects changing in shape and size.

LSD can produce strange hallucinations.

In about two hours he felt normal again. We now know that he had accidentally been exposed to a drug called *LSD*, which was present in the chemicals he was working with. Like marijuana it is a hallucinogen. Unlike marijuana this drug is so strong that Dr. Hofmann had gotten enough to produce strong effects without even knowing he had taken anything.

LSD—or *LSD-25*, as it is sometimes called—is an abbreviation for the chemical name, lysergic acid diethylamide. Users call it simply *"acid,"* and they call themselves *"acid heads."* The drug is made from the chemical lysergic acid, which occurs in the ergot fungus.

Although the drug has been known for over twenty years, it is only recently that people have started taking it for other than scientific purposes.

LSD has no color, taste, or odor, and it is usually taken by mouth. It is extremely powerful. Five-millionths of an ounce (about as much as a grain of salt) can make someone have full hallucinations. One half ounce (about a tablespoon full) would be enough to make 100,000 people have hallucinations.

Medical uses

Many doctors and scientists have tried to find out whether LSD has any use in treating diseases. They have tried it on certain mental patients and on alcoholics. Some of them have found that it is quite useful, yet others have found that it has little value. As a medical treatment it still needs more study, and at this time it has no accepted medical use in this country.

Effects

LSD produces its main effects on the brain and other parts of the nervous system. The nervous system in turn makes changes in other parts of the body. These changes are similar to what happens when a person gets very scared or angry. The heartbeat speeds up and the blood pressure increases. The pupils of the eyes get large, and the body temperature goes up. The hands shake and the person may have chills and shiver. He may feel sick to his stomach and lose his appetite. If he takes a very high dose, he may have convulsions, in which his arms and legs jerk around uncontrollably.

It is not the body changes that interest the LSD user, however. The drug also produces extraordinary effects on the mind, and these are the effects the user seeks.

A low dose of LSD makes a user feel strange and unusual. He laughs or cries easily. He may feel nervous and jumpy. A larger dose may produce a

NEXT PAGE: Friends at a party may look weird and distorted to the person who has taken LSD.

feeling of well-being and pleasure. A still higher dose affects the user's senses—his sight, feeling, taste, hearing, and smell. Floors and ceilings seem to move. Colors seem brighter. Strange patterns may appear. Flat things may suddenly seem to have three dimensions. Sense impressions overlap, so that music seems to have colors or colors seem to have a taste. Everything may look incredibly beautiful, or horrible. The user often feels happy and sad at the same time. His arms and legs may feel both heavy and light.

One student described an experience with LSD as follows: "Like I was sitting there, in the classroom, and like the tiles on the floor were waving. Seaweed was growing up, up out of the floor. It was fantastic and I was just sitting back digging it and the teacher walked into the room and he sat down at his desk and all these flames came up around him. What was really freaky was that he was so normal but I kept seeing him in these flames and everything, and he was like sitting there and talking to the class, with all these flames coming out of his head. And then the flames started coming back toward me. I asked to get a drink of water and got out of the room."

A large dose may cause a user to feel that he is no longer part of his own body. He may look at his hands and feet and feel that they are not part of him. One user said that he looked into a mirror and felt that his reflection was his true self and he was the

50

reflection. Still greater amounts of the drug can cause full hallucinations. The user will see and hear people and things that are not there, and he will not even realize that the drug is causing them. To him they are real, and they are often extremely frightening. This state is called a *psychosis* or *psychotic reaction*. A similar state occurs in some severe types of mental illness.

Characteristics of abuse

LSD does not produce physical dependence, the way heroin does. The user does not get withdrawal illness when he stops using the drug. But it may lead to psychological dependence. The user's mind can develop a need for the drug, as it can for marijuana.

Tolerance to LSD develops fast, however. After the drug has been used daily for only a few days, tolerance develops and the user has to increase the dose to get the same effects. But tolerance also disappears quickly when the user stops taking the drug. After a few days without the drug, the user can get the same effects from a small dose as he did the first time he took it. Usually an LSD user does not take the drug often enough to build up much tolerance.

Since LSD is so powerful, it is easy for users to conceal the small amounts they need. Often they dissolve small amounts in water and then soak a cube of sugar, a cookie, or a stick of chewing gum it in. Sometimes they put the drug on the back of a postage stamp, and then lick the back of the stamp. Because LSD must be bought illegally and is practically impossible to identify, the user is never sure what he is getting. There is evidence that much black-market LSD is being "cut" with other substances. Some of these are even more dangerous and poisonous drugs.

As with marijuana-smoking, the setting in which people take LSD will strongly influence the type of effects it produces. Some people take LSD in a religious setting, and feel that the drug lets them talk with God. Others, particularly artists, claim that LSD increases their sensitivity and helps them to be more creative. There is no scientific evidence to support such claims.

The emotional state of the user is also important. Sometimes the hallucinations produced by the drug can be terrifying. They can lead to a state of panic, which users refer to as a *bad trip*. It is impossible to foresee the type of person, the setting, or the mood that will result in a bad trip. A person can have a hundred good trips and then a bad one. This is one girl's description of a bad trip:

"I was in the girls' locker room and I thought I heard the water running so I went over to the showers. The showers weren't really on, but I saw water pouring down. The water on the floor kept coming up higher and higher and I thought I was drowning. I was treading water to try to keep alive and then I passed out. When I came to, I still didn't know what was happening. I still thought there was water all around me."

Such psychotic reactions can happen to anyone if he takes enough of the drug, and they can lead to disastrous results. Some people have been killed because they got the idea that they could fly and jumped off a roof. One man, thinking he was Superman, tried to stop a freight train by standing on the tracks and holding up his hand. There is no way of telling how sensitive any particular person is going to be to LSD. Also, a user's sensitivity can change without warning. He can take the same dose over and over again, feeling only mild effects, and then suddenly have a psychotic reaction from the same dose.

The effects of a usual dose of LSD are usually gone in about eight hours. In some cases, however, they can last much longer. Nobody knows the reason for these long reactions. They are usually of the bad-trip type, and often the victim has to be treated in a hospital. It may take him months to recover.

LSD can also bring on other disturbed emotional states. It sometimes makes people extremely nervous or unhappy. These moods can take a long time to wear off, perhaps months.

In addition to these dangers, LSD users run the

The beginning of a bad trip.

risk of having what they call a *"return trip."* This means that they have the sensations of an acid trip without having taken anything. It can happen even as long as six months after their last trip. These return trips, or *flashbacks,* come without any warning, and sometimes more than once. This can be the most terrifying of all drug experiences, because the sufferer may be convinced that he has lost his mind.

Scientists have recently been studying the possible effects of LSD on the parts of the human cells that control inheritance, called *chromosomes.* Damage to chromosomes may in some instances lead to birth defects. So far their experiments have produced conflicting results. Some show damage to chromosomes, others show no effects. The reasons for these different results are not yet understood, and the possible effects of LSD on inheritance and birth defects are still being investigated and are not definitely known at this time.

Like other drugs that are not used for medical purposes, LSD is illegal. It is against the law to have it, to buy or sell it, or to give it away. Anyone who does so risks being sent to jail.

Other hallucinogens

Many of the effects produced by LSD are the same for other hallucinogenic drugs. One of these is *peyote,* which is a mixture of drugs found in a certain cactus. This plant grows in deserts, including those of this country. The drug in peyote that produces the effects is called *mescaline.*

Psilocybin is another hallucinogen. It comes from a mushroom. Its effects and dangers are also similar to LSD.

Other hallucinogens can be made from simple chemicals. These are usually known by the initials of their chemical name. The most common are *DOM, STP, DET, DMT,* and *DOET.* Their effects, similar to those of LSD, are not well known yet.

5 Sedatives

The *sedatives* are a group of drugs that lessen the activity of the brain and other parts of the body. They have the ability to calm people and to produce sleep.

This is a large category of drugs. For purposes of discussion they may be broken down into two large classes: the *barbiturates* and the *non-barbiturates*. The non-barbiturates may be further divided into the *major tranquilizers* and the *minor tranquilizers*.

The major tranquilizers are a group of potent drugs used in the treatment of certain mental illnesses. They are not common drugs of abuse. Some of the minor tranquilizers, however, constitute a major problem of abuse.

In the rest of this chapter the word "sedative" will be used to mean those barbiturates and minor tranquilizers that are frequently abused. Although there are some differences between barbiturates and minor tranquilizers, their main effects are the same. In addition, they are all manufactured from simple chemicals rather than coming from plants.

The barbiturates are popularly known as sleeping pills. Slang names for the group as a whole include such terms as *barbs, goof balls, downs,* and *downers.* Some of the most commonly abused barbiturates are shown in Table 1. The slang names listed there for individual drugs often refer to the color of the capsules.

Some of the commonly abused minor tranquilizers are shown in Table 2. Slang names for these individual drugs are not often used.

Medical uses

Sedatives are used in small amounts to treat people who are nervous and excited. They are also useful to calm patients with certain heart diseases or stomach ulcers. The sedatives are very useful when used for a short period (perhaps a few weeks) ac-

Commonly Abused Barbiturates   Table 1

GENERIC NAME (common name)	TRADE NAME	SLANG NAME
phenobarbital	Luminal	idiot pills, feenies
amobarbital	Amytal	blue heaven
pentobarbital	Nembutal	yellow jackets
secobarbital	Seconal	red devils, red birds, reds, pinks, Seggys
combination of amobarbital and secobarbital	Tuinal	Christmas trees, rainbows, Tooies

Commonly Abused Minor Tranquilizers   Table 2

GENERIC NAME (common name)	TRADE NAME
meprobamate	Miltown, Equanil
glutethimide	Doriden
chlordiazepoxide	Librium
diazepam	Valium
methprylon	Noludar
ethchlorvinal	Placidyl

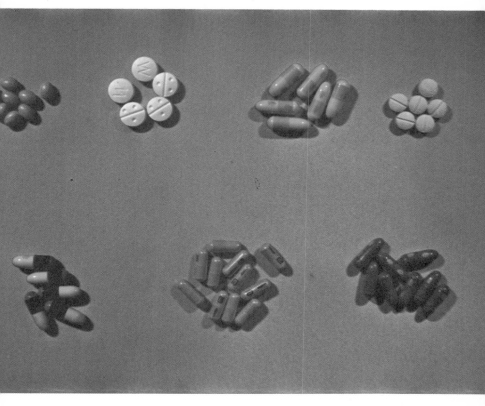

A selection of some of the sedatives listed in the tables.

cording to a doctor's instructions, to get people over troublesome situations and help them get to sleep. In addition, because of their ability to lessen brain activity, these drugs are useful in treating epilepsy, a disease in which convulsions occur.

Effects

In low doses the sedatives calm or *sedate*. In high doses they put people to sleep. In very high doses they produce additional effects such as a lessening of breathing and making the action of the heart weaker.

People who abuse these drugs take them in much higher doses than doctors normally prescribe. In such large doses they make people drunk, as alcohol does. The user's speech is slurred, he staggers, and he loses control of his emotions. There is a decrease in his ability to think and make sound judgments. Here is how one girl described some of her schoolmates who took sedatives: "Oh, the down heads, those are the ones that walk around and they're very sleepy-eyed. They just walk around and say 'Wow, I'm stoned.' "

Because of these effects, people under the influence of sedatives can have accidents or get into fights. In very high doses these drugs may produce coma and death.

"They just walk around and say 'Wow, I'm stoned.'"

Characteristics of abuse

Continued heavy use of sedatives produces tolerance and both psychological and physical dependence. However, tolerance to the sedatives does not develop to nearly the same degree as it does to narcotics. For example, the sedative addict may have increased his dosage ten times, but a heroin addict may use fifty times the original amount or even more. The sickness which develops when the drug is suddenly stopped after taking it for a long time is particularly dangerous. It begins with weakness, anxiety, inability to sleep, and tremor (shakiness in the muscles). If not treated, this sickness can go on to convulsions and a mental state known as *delirium*. In this state a person gets very excited, has hallucinations, and loses contact with reality. During this time he can become totally exhausted and sometimes even die.

One teen-age girl described an experience with a friend. "My boy friend was taking pills for a long, long time—constantly, every day and every night, a lot of them. And when you stop, you know, you get seizures. This isn't with every person. I didn't get seizures or anything; he did. It's sort of similar to an epileptic attack. Like he fell down, he was in his pantry and he fell down. His father's a doctor. His father knew what to do. He was rolling all around and they had to hold his tongue down so he didn't swallow it. When they revived him, he didn't remember anything that happened."

The withdrawal illness from sedatives may be a threat to life. It can be treated, with a doctor's supervision, by gradually reducing the drug, not taking it away suddenly. Recovery is slow, taking perhaps up to six months. As far as we know, recovery is complete.

Like some other drugs we have talked about, sedatives are often used by people attempting to escape from their troubles. The drugs make them feel calm and confident, and they forget about their problems for the time being.

These drugs are used by doctors in the treatment of severe anxiety, nervousness, and difficulty in sleeping, but one must be extremely careful to use them only with adequate medical supervision. Since sedatives are widely prescribed and easily available, a person may fall into the habit of depending on them for the relief of minor emotional upsets and everyday stresses and problems. This kind of use may lead to psychological dependence and even to physical dependence.

The sedatives are sometimes abused along with other drugs such as narcotics and alcohol. Such combinations are very dangerous. The effect of both drugs together is often unpredictable and may be greater than the effect of each drug alone.

Abuse of sedatives can result in an accidental overdose. These drugs are usually taken by swallowing pills, and it may be as long as half an hour before any effect is felt. A person sometimes gets impatient waiting for the effects to begin, and takes more and more pills. By the time the effects do begin, he may already have taken enough to kill himself. Sedatives can also make a person confused, so that he forgets how much drug he has already taken. In this state of mind, he might take a very large and dangerous amount without realizing it.

Still another hazard of sedatives is their ability to produce a kind of drunkenness, similar to that produced by alcohol. Fights and accidents often result when people are under such sedative influence— and this can be very harmful not only to themselves but to other people as well.

Stimulants 6

Stimulants are drugs that increase the activity of the brain and other parts of the nervous system. There are a large number of stimulants, belonging to several different chemical classes.

Some are quite weak. For example the caffeine in coffee is one of a group of stimulants called *xanthines*. Xanthines are also found in tea, cocoa, and colas. Since the xanthines are so mild, not many people misuse them. It is quite safe to take moderate amounts of these drinks.

Cocaine is another stimulant. It occurs naturally, in coca leaves. It used to be a commonly abused stimulant, but now it has become quite expensive. New drugs, from a different chemical class but with many similar effects, can be bought more cheaply, and these are widely abused today.

These new drugs, called *amphetamines,* are all made from simple chemicals. The most commonly misused stimulants are shown in Table 3, with their generic (common), trade, and slang names. Slang names for the whole class of drugs are also shown in the last column. By far the most popular stimulants for abuse are *Benzedrine, Dexedrine,* and *Methedrine.*

Medical uses

Doctors have prescribed amphetamines since the 1930s for medical purposes. They are used to treat several diseases of the nervous system. Most often, however, they are used to help people lose weight, because they cut down the appetite. They are frequently called diet pills. Many dieters take pills that combine amphetamines and barbiturates. The barbiturate in the pill keeps the amphetamine from making the patient too jumpy, but his appetite is still lessened.

Doctors have also used amphetamines to pep people up or to make them more cheerful if they were sad or depressed. Better drugs are now available

GENERIC NAME (common name)	TRADE NAME	SLANG NAME	
		SPECIFIC	GENERAL
d,l-amphetamine	Benzedrine	bennies, hearts, cartwheels, peaches	speed, wake-ups, pep pills, ups, uppers, co-pilots, lid-poppers
d-amphetamine	Dexedrine	dexes, hearts, oranges	
methamphetamine	Methedrine Desoxyn	speed, crystals	
methylphenidate	Ritalin		
phenmetrazine	Preludin		
combinations of d- and d,l-amphetamine	Biphetamine	B-20's, black beauty	

for most of these purposes, and the amphetamines are now seldom prescribed in such cases.

Effects

With usual doses of amphetamines, the physical effects are not severe. These drugs may increase the blood pressure, and at first speed up and then slow down the heart beat. They lessen appetite. They also wake people up—in large enough doses, they can keep people awake for several days at a time. They seem to increase the ability to perform simple mental tasks.

When a person takes an amphetamine pill, he feels alert, happy, and full of self-confidence and physical and mental power. The pill peps him up and takes away any feeling of tiredness he might have had. He becomes very active. Tired truck drivers often use them to keep themselves alert. Students take them when they are cramming for exams. Although it is strictly against the rules of all organized sports, athletes sometimes take them before competing.

When a dose of amphetamine is injected directly into a person's veins, he gets all the effects he would get from a pill, but he also feels a state of intense physical and mental pleasure. Users call this feeling a rush. It occurs within seconds of the injection and lasts for only a few minutes. This is how one user described how he felt after shooting (injecting) some speed (amphetamine): "What did I get out of shooting speed? A flash. It's like a rush of white light, and a buzzing sound in the back of my head that I enjoy." This feeling is one of the main reasons that people abuse amphetamines.

In large doses amphetamines may make a person confused and anxious, and they may affect his vision. Such effects are dangerous. For example, when people take large doses to stay awake while driving, they may get into accidents. One truck driver jack-knifed his tractor trailer while he was on amphetamines. He said he had been trying to escape from a large imaginary serpent that was wriggling into his cab.

Characteristics of abuse

Like all the other drugs mentioned so far, amphetamines may lead to psychological dependence, and tolerance to some of the physical effects. Physical dependence may or may not develop—doctors are not yet sure about this.

People who misuse amphetamines fall into two groups, according to how they take the drugs.

The first group is made up of people who take the drug by mouth, in the form of pills. Some take it

NEXT PAGE: Large doses of amphetamine may cause visual distortion, which can make driving extremely dangerous.

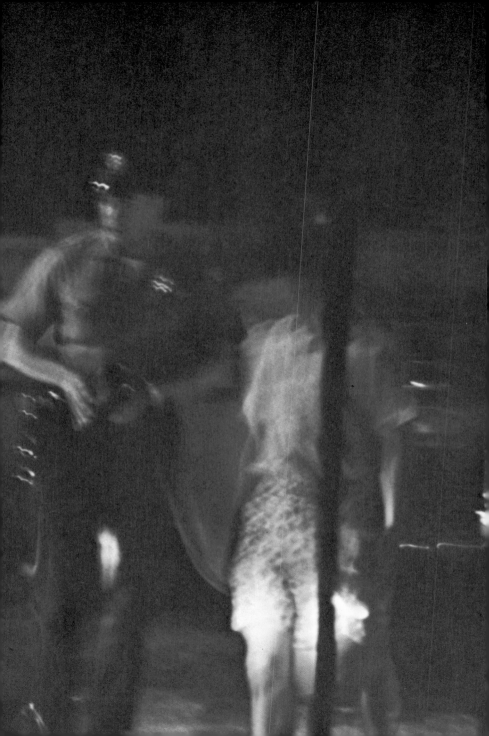

only occasionally—for example, on weekends—and others use it every day. After a while they develop tolerance and a psychological need for the drug.

All are usually seeking the feeling of well-being, self-confidence, and energy that the drugs give them. However, they can also get nervous, restless, and irritable. They have a hard time eating and sleeping, and lose weight. Their heartbeat is rapid and uneven. The pupils of their eyes are enlarged, and their arms and legs shake.

After taking large doses of the drug for a long time, they can become mentally disturbed in a way that makes them believe people are plotting against them and trying to hurt them. This state is called *paranoid psychosis*. It can make a person very dangerous. He may fight or even kill innocent people, because he thinks they are trying to hurt him. This type of behavior is what most people think of when they picture a "dope fiend."

Some abusers of stimulants take them along with sedatives. They will take a stimulant to get them "up" (or excited), and then, when they feel they are too "high," they take a sedative to calm down. When they begin to feel too "low," they take a stimulant again. They continue this way, "up" and "down" like a seesaw.

Like sedatives, amphetamines should be used only under a doctor's care. People using ampheta-

mines to help them with dieting may find the stimulating effects pleasant, and if they are not careful,
they may find themselves becoming dependent on the
drug to relieve tiredness and boredom.

The second group of people who abuse amphetamines are those who inject the drugs directly into
their veins. Doctors call this *I.V.* or *intravenous* use.
Users call it *shooting*. I.V. use is becoming a very
big and dangerous problem.

A typical I.V. user is young and part of a drug-
taking crowd. He starts out by taking pills, and only
injects the drug once in a while. After a period of
time, he may go on to try what is called a "run"—
he tries to maintain a state of intense mental and
physical pleasure by using amphetamines. He injects
the drug frequently, as often as every two hours. As
tolerance develops, he increases the size of the dose.
Day and night he continues, increasing the dose and
injecting it more often. The run usually lasts from
five to six days.

At the end, the user is injecting up to forty times
the normal dose, at very frequent intervals. One girl
gave herself 100 injections in one 24-hour period.
This means that she was taking an average of one
dose every fifteen minutes.

At the end of five or six days the user becomes
so exhausted, nervous, or mentally disturbed that he
stops taking the drug. What follows is a reaction

called "crashing." He falls into a deep sleep, which usually lasts from twelve to eighteen hours but can last as long as two days. When he wakes up he is very hungry and very depressed. To get away from these feelings, he starts on another run.

The user who shoots amphetamines has to face bad results. He can get the same kind of severe infection from using dirty needles as the heroin user. During a run he sleeps and eats very little. He becomes totally exhausted and, in time, malnourished and very thin. One boy put it this way. "After, I'd say, about the first six months, that's when I was a total wreck. I lost about forty pounds and my whole body was emaciated. When I really got into drugs, I stopped taking care of myself. And that's what happened to me—like my cheekbones would be sticking out, and my ribs, and I was all distorted. I felt like everybody was my enemy. I was scared that I'd flip out and never come back."

I.V. users develop paranoid psychosis much more often than users who take pills. As a result, they can become involved in senseless violence and even murder. It is also possible that amphetamines can permanently damage the brain. Some people have found that they have trouble remembering things, even after they have been off the drug for a long time. In addition, accidental overdoses of amphetamines have sometimes resulted in death.

Alcohol, the Legal Drug 7

Out of approximately 200 million people in the United States, it is estimated that 80 million drink alcohol in one form or another. Of these, perhaps 6 to 8 million could be considered chronic alcohol abusers, unproductive and a problem to society.

In this chapter, the word *alcohol* refers to a simple chemical compound called ethyl alcohol, or grain alcohol. Alcohol is a *depressant,* similar in many respects to the sedatives. It decreases the activity of the brain and other parts of the body.

Unlike all the other drugs we have talked about, alcohol can be used for nonmedical purposes without

Most towns have at least one liquor store.

breaking a law. It may be bought without a doctor's prescription in almost every part of the United States —and throughout most of the world. In some states 18-year-olds may buy alcohol; in most states the legal age is 21.

Alcohol is taken into the body in the form of liquids. *Rum, gin, vodka, brandy, rye, bourbon,* and *Scotch* contain the greatest amount of alcohol. *Wine* has about one-quarter as much as these per ounce, and *beer* about one-tenth as much.

Alcohol goes into the bloodstream very rapidly from the stomach and small intestine. This process is called *absorption.* The rate of absorption from the stomach can be influenced by many factors. If you have eaten something and then take a drink, the alcohol will be absorbed more slowly than if your stomach were empty. Also, the ability to absorb alcohol differs somewhat from person to person.

As the alcohol enters the bloodstream, it is carried to the brain and other parts of the body. The amount of alcohol in the bloodstream determines how much effect it will have on the brain and body, and that amount depends on how much is being absorbed and how much is being excreted and broken down by the body.

The amount of alcohol absorbed over any period of time depends also on such factors as how much alcohol is in the drink and how fast it is drunk. For example, a person drinking whiskey rapidly on an empty stomach will feel a faster and greater effect than a person drinking beer slowly after a large meal. The widespread idea that "mixing your drinks" (for example, drinking beer and then wine) brings a greater effect than drinking a single beverage, is a misconception. The amount of alcohol in the bloodstream is the important factor—not the particular beverage, or mixture of beverages, consumed.

The body gets rid of alcohol in two ways. A small amount, less than 10 percent, is excreted through the kidneys (via the urine) and the lungs (in the breath). The majority of the alcohol is destroyed by the body in a way similar to the utilization of food, a process called *metabolism*.

The body has the ability to use about one-half ounce of pure alcohol per hour as food. If only one-half ounce of alcohol is drunk in an hour the body destroys it about as rapidly as it is absorbed. One-half ounce of pure alcohol is about equal to an ounce of whiskey, or a 4-ounce glass of wine, or one 12-ounce can of beer. With this quantity of alcohol, the level in the blood remains very low and there are only very slight effects. One-half ounce of alcohol has about the same number of *calories* as one hot dog. Just as in absorption, individuals also differ somewhat in the speed with which their bodies can metabolize alcohol.

Besides the amount of alcohol in the blood, the mood and experience of the drinker, and the situation he is in, may all alter an individual's reaction to alcohol. For example, a person drinking alone may react quite differently from one at a party. A person who is sad and lonely may find that alcohol makes him sadder and lonelier. A person in a happy mood may become happier when he drinks.

Medical uses

Although alcohol is a depressant drug, it is seldom used in modern medical practice as a sedative. Barbiturates and minor tranquilizers are more reliable sedatives, and their effects can be more easily predicted by the doctor.

Alcohol is often used medically to dissolve drugs that do not dissolve in water, so that they can be taken by mouth and easily absorbed from the stomach and intestines. Many cough mixtures are examples of this use of alcohol. Alcohol is also widely used to sterilize or disinfect (that is, to kill the germs on) the skin and other surfaces, such as medical instruments and table tops.

Effects

Many people think of alcohol as a stimulating drug. This is not correct. It is a depressant.

One way we normally control our behavior is by restraining ourselves. That is, we keep ourselves from doing things we have learned are wrong or not appropriate to the situation. Since alcohol depresses the parts of the brain that control our behavior, people may do things under the influence of alcohol that they usually would not do. For example, if someone in a discussion said something that made you very angry, you might feel like hitting him. But since you know that this is no way to settle the discussion, you restrain yourself. Under the influence of alcohol, however, you might go ahead and start a fight. This would not be because alcohol had stimulated or excited you, but because it slowed down the parts of your brain you use to control your actions.

Other kinds of unrestrained behavior produced by alcohol are shown by people who become unusually talkative, loud-mouthed, gay, or carefree. Alcohol may make one feel relaxed, and this can lead to feelings of great self-confidence and ability, but alcohol does not actually increase anyone's mental or physical abilities. In fact, it will decrease your ability to coordinate your muscles, to make correct judgments, to keep your balance, and to speak clearly. It decreases the ability to concentrate and interferes with clear thinking.

Alcohol can make you moody, so that one moment you are very happy and the next very sad.

What starts as a friendly get-together can end in a fight.

Emotional outbursts, like fighting or crying jags, are also common occurrences under the influence of alcohol. One girl, talking about what it was like to live with an alcoholic father, said: "He used to get very violent. He used to come after us, every night. He used to come home and, you know, try to set the house on fire, or go through numbers like 'I'm going to kill you,' or throw knives back and forth, and everybody used to be in a whole outrage all through the whole night. Every night."

Alcohol causes the blood vessels in the skin to become larger, giving a feeling of warmth. This has led to the myth that drinking alcohol will warm you up when you are cold. However, the effect of alcohol on the blood vessels means that the body loses its heat quickly. Although a drinker feels warmer for a short time, his body is really getting colder.

Alcohol also irritates the lining of the stomach. This is why drinking frequently leads to nausea and vomiting.

The immediate effects of alcohol are referred to as *drunkenness* or being drunk. As a person drinks more and more, the level of alcohol in his blood increases, and he may pass out. At very high blood levels, alcohol can cause death, by depressing the part of the brain that controls breathing.

"Sobering up" means recovering from the effects

of drunkenness. Unfortunately, there is no quick way to do this. Dousing your head in cold water or drinking a few cups of coffee will not sober you up. It might make you feel a little more alert, but your coordination and balance and judgment will still be affected. The only sure way to sober up is to wait until your body has excreted and destroyed all the alcohol you have drunk. After sobering up, a drinker often has an illness called a *"hangover."* This usually consists of a queasy stomach, a headache, and a general achy and sick feeling. Nobody knows exactly what causes this condition, and there is no special treatment for it but time. The hangover will wear off in a few hours.

Characteristics of abuse

The behavior of people under the influence of alcohol can be dangerous both to themselves and to others. Falls resulting in injury are quite common, because of the effect on balance and coordination of the muscles. The greatest single danger, however, is an automobile driver who has been drinking. One study showed that a drunken driver is 33 times more likely to have an automobile accident than a driver who has not been drinking. The National Highway Safety Bureau feels that drunkenness is responsible for at least one-half of all deaths from automobile

Drinking causes nearly a million serious traffic accidents on American streets and highways each year.

accidents. They estimate that drunken drivers and drunken pedestrians cause 800,000 serious accidents and 25,000 deaths every year in this country.

Some people try to escape from their troubles by drinking constantly. Chronic heavy drinkers, called *alcoholics,* develop both physical and psychological dependence and some tolerance to the drug.

The alcoholic's sole purpose in life becomes getting more and more alcohol. He is often unable to hold a job, and unable to be a good member of his family. Often he does not get enough food and becomes undernourished, because he lacks interest in eating and sometimes because he has spent all he has to buy liquor. He is frequently in trouble with the law.

Alcoholism brings many serious physical consequences. It damages the liver, the brain (including the memory functions), the stomach, and the nerves, and some of the damage is permanent. Furthermore, an alcoholic often does not have enough money to buy expensive liquor, so he will drink whatever he can get hold of. Because of this he risks being poisoned by another form of alcohol, called *methanol.* A small quantity of methanol can cause blindness and death. Poisoning can also occur from drinking rubbing alcohol, known chemically as *isopropanol.*

When an alcoholic suddenly stops drinking, withdrawal illness results. This sickness is very similar to the one that results from suddenly stopping barbiturates after prolonged abuse. It can bring on delirium and convulsions, which sometimes lead to death. The alcoholic's withdrawal illness is commonly called the *"D.T.'s,"* which stands for *delirium tremens.* The patient has shakiness in his arms and legs. He is nervous, weak, and unable to sleep. He may become very excited and have vivid hallucinations. He may also become totally exhausted, develop a very high fever, and even die if he doesn't get medical treatment.

Alcoholism is not a hopeless disease. There are many agencies with treatment programs, and they have had success in helping alcoholics back to normal lives.

To drink or not to drink?

It is not the purpose of this chapter to tell you that you should or should not drink. This is a decision each of you will make at some time and perhaps a decision you will have to make early in your high-school years. Your decision will be influenced by many factors. For example, your friends, your home, and your religion may all play a part.

Some teen-agers choose not to drink. They may not like the taste, or the effect, or the custom of using alcoholic beverages. They may be going along with parents' wishes, a girl friend's or boy friend's preferences, athletic training rules, or their crowd's habits. If you choose not to drink, it may be difficult to say "no" when others are drinking, but if your choice is well thought out, you should be able to stand behind it. Respect the choice of others and expect them to respect yours.

Some people decide in favor of drinking. They may enjoy the beverage, or the effect, or being accepted in a certain group, or making the choice on their own. Some may be rebelling against their parents, and others may be following their family customs.

Whatever you decide on one occasion, you might change your mind later. If you drink at all, obey the laws concerning drinking. Understand the effects and dangers of alcohol and learn to use it wisely. Don't drink to get drunk, or to show off, or to escape your cares and troubles. Limit yourself to a few drinks well spread out. Never drive an automobile when you have been drinking. Respect the choice of non-drinkers not to drink.

8 Other Drugs

The practice of *glue-sniffing* is the cause of increasing concern among parents, doctors, and educators. The deliberate and potentially dangerous inhaling of fumes from glue and other substances, for the purpose of producing a drunken-like state, is apparently being tried by thousands of youngsters.

The substances in glue that produce a "high" are called *organic solvents*. These solvents are used in a variety of products. They evaporate easily and give off vapor that can be breathed in and absorbed quickly into the bloodstream. The products most commonly abused are plastic cements, fingernail polish remover, lighter and cleaning fluid, and gasoline. The chemicals *toluene, acetone,* and *benzene* are the most common solvents in these products.

The effects of vapor from organic solvents differ slightly from chemical to chemical. The physical effects are different for different people, and the situation and the emotional make-up of the user can also influence the effects. When a person sniffs glue he feels powerful, self-confident, and generally good— at first. This phase is called a *"jag."* At this time, some people experience distortion of the senses and even hallucinations, and this can get them into fights or accidents—sometimes fatal. When someone keeps on sniffing, he begins to feel the depressant effect of the solvents. He may stagger and slur his speech as if he were drunk. He can have double vision, a buzzing in the ears, or a headache, and he may feel sick to his stomach. These effects usually last half or three-quarters of an hour. Then he gets drowsy and may fall asleep for an hour or more. Higher doses can put him in a coma or kill him.

If a person sniffs glue for a long time, he can build up psychological dependence and tolerance. Some users sniff up to 25 tubes of glue a day. Physical dependence on organic solvents probably does not occur, but scientists are not sure about that yet.

Students who spend a lot of time sniffing glue usually begin to do badly in school. They are often

absent and sometimes drop out altogether. They often start stealing in order to get enough money to buy glue to support their habit.

It is not dangerous to use glue and products with organic solvents for the purposes for which they were intended. Of course, it is impossible not to breathe in some vapor, but in normal use not enough is absorbed to be dangerous. The glue-sniffer takes in much more vapor. He usually soaks a sock or a handkerchief in glue and then puts it close to his face in order to get the strongest possible fumes. Often he puts the soaked cloth in a plastic bag and then puts the bag over his mouth and nose, and sometimes he suffocates this way for lack of air.

The vapor irritates the linings of his mouth, nose, and lungs. This leads to coughing, sneezing, and pains in the chest. Constant glue-sniffing may also damage certain organs of the body. Studies in animals have shown that organic solvents may damage the brain, liver, kidneys, and bone marrow.

Drug-taking is getting so popular that some children try to outdo each other in efforts to get a different kind of high. They experiment with anything they hear about or can think of. They completely ignore the terrible risks they may be taking, partly because they are too young to understand them. One girl, describing what was going on in her school, said,

Vapors from organic solvents can cause hallucinations.

"They'd try anything. They'd try aspirin if someone handed it to them and said, 'Wow, here, this is really fantastic.' And just the other day I heard about this thing called a punch party. All the kids clean out their parents' medicine chests, throw everything into a bowl, and then they just pick whatever they want. They have no idea what they're taking. I mean they could be taking a laxative, for all they know, or a yeast pill."

Other kids are trying anything from morning-glory seeds to peanut-butter oil to see what it will do. They may try something because they have heard a rumor that it is good. They may hear, for example, that an ancient Indian tribe used a certain plant in religious rituals. Then they have to try the plant for themselves.

The effects they usually seek are excitement, drunkenness, sensory distortions, and hallucinations. Often they take something without having any knowledge of it at all. Psychological factors, such as the emotional state of the user and what he may expect to feel, play a large part in the feelings he does get. As one girl said, "You can get a high from Seven-Up if someone tells you there's something in it." Little if anything is known about the dangers of many of the things they take. Many young people get terribly sick and even die from experimenting with them.

"They'd try anything."

9
It's Your Decision

The pressures of life in our society create problems for everybody. Children growing up may feel pressures at school and have difficulty getting along with their parents and friends. Adults worry about their jobs, their friends, and their families. It is natural for everyone to want some pleasure, relaxation, and friendship—and to be part of a crowd. It is normal for young people to question and even to rebel against authority, and to be concerned about injustice and inequality. Young people also want to grow and expand their knowledge and abilities.

An increasing number have been turning to drugs to help them with their troubles. Instead of

thinking about what their problems really are and trying to find ways to deal with them, they take drugs in order to forget about them. But they often find that they then have worse problems than before.

Some people take drugs for kicks and to find acceptance and friendship. But the kicks do not last long, and the friendships made on this basis turn out to be shallow and insincere.

Rather than working to correct injustice and inequality in our society, some people express their disgust by dropping out of society altogether. This does nothing to change society for the better.

Some people use drugs hoping to expand their knowledge and capabilities. But there is little evidence that the drugs really can do this.

You will probably hear more about drugs. It is very likely that you will be exposed to them sometime, at school or on the street. You may be tempted to try them, and have to make a choice.

Saying "no" can be terribly hard. You may feel that you might lose your friends if they take drugs and you don't want to. Unfortunately, this may be true. You may be able to convince your friends not to use drugs, but you may just have to find other friends, who are not deeply involved in the world of drugs. Learn all you can about drugs. Understand the dangers and consequences of drug abuse. In the end the decision will be yours.

Glossary

absorption

The passage of a substance from the stomach and intestine into the bloodstream.

acetone

An organic solvent.

acid

Slang name for LSD.

acid head

Slang name for a heavy user of LSD.

alcohol

Usually, the chemical ethyl alcohol (or grain alcohol), which is a depressant drug.

alcoholic

One who drinks alcohol heavily and continuously.

alcoholism
Physical and psychological dependence on alcohol.

amobarbital
Common name for a barbiturate with the trade name Amytal.

amphetamines
A large class of stimulants made from simple chemicals.

Amytal
Trade name for the barbiturate amobarbital.

antibiotic
A medicine used to treat infections.

B-20's
A slang name for a combination of amphetamines with the trade name Biphetamine.

bad trip
An LSD experience in which the drug· effects are unpleasant and sometimes frightening.

barbiturates
A large class of sedative drugs.

barbs
A slang name for barbiturates.

beer
An alcoholic beverage made from malt.

bennies
A slang name for Benzedrine.

Benzedrine
Trade name for d,l-amphetamine, a stimulant drug.

benzene

An organic solvent.

bhang

Slang name for a drink made from the leaves of the Indian hemp plant.

Biphetamine

Trade name for a combination of d- and d,l-amphetamine.

black beauty

A slang name for a combination of amphetamines with the trade name Biphetamine.

blue heaven

Slang name for a barbiturate with the trade name Amytal.

bourbon

An alcoholic beverage made from corn.

brandy

An alcoholic beverage made from fruit.

calorie

A measurement of food energy.

cartwheels

A slang name for Benzedrine.

chlordiazepoxide

Common name for a minor tranquilizer with the trade name Librium.

Christmas trees

A slang name for a combination of barbiturates with the trade name Tuinal.

chromosomes

The parts of human reproductive cells that control inheritance.

coasting

A slang term for the kind of light sleep that follows the immediate effects of heroin; often accompanied by "nodding."

cocaine

A stimulant drug derived from coca leaves.

codeine

A narcotic drug made from opium.

co-pilots

A slang name for stimulant drugs.

crystals

A slang name for methamphetamine with the trade name Methedrine.

cutting

A slang term for mixing a drug, usually a narcotic, with other substances to make it go farther.

d-amphetamine

Common name for an amphetamine with the trade name Dexedrine.

d,l-amphetamine

Common name for Benzedrine.

delirium

A disturbed mental state in which a person may be very excited, have hallucinations, and lose touch with reality.

delirium tremens

The name given to the alcoholic's withdrawal illness.

Demerol

Trade name for the narcotic drug meperidine.

depressants

Drugs that slow down the activity of the brain and other parts of the body.

Desoxyn

A trade name for methamphetamine.

DET

Commonly used abbreviation for one of the hallucinogenic drugs made from simple chemicals.

Dexedrine

Trade name for d-amphetamine, a stimulant in the amphetamine class.

dexes

A slang name for Dexedrine.

diazepam

Common name for a minor tranquilizer with the trade name Valium.

DMT

Commonly used abbreviation for one of the hallucinogenic drugs made from simple chemicals.

DOET

Commonly used abbreviation for one of the hallucinogenic drugs made from simple chemicals.

Dolophine

Trade name for the narcotic drug methadone.

DOM

Commonly used abbreviation for one of the hallucinogenic drugs made from simple chemicals.

Doriden

Trade name for the minor tranquilizer glutethimide.

downers, downs

Slang names for sedatives.

drug

Broadly speaking, any substance that affects living matter; usually, a substance used in treating illness or relieving pain.

drug abuse

The use of a drug for purposes other than treating sickness, often leading to serious harm.

drug addict

A person who is physically or psychologically dependent on a drug.

drug effect

A change produced by a drug.

drunkenness

The immediate effects of alcohol.

D.T.'s

A slang abbreviation for delirium tremens, the name given to the alcoholic's withdrawal illness.

Equanil

A trade name for the minor tranquilizer meprobamate.

ethchlorvinal

Common name for a minor tranquilizer with the trade name Placidyl.

feenies

A slang name for a barbiturate with the trade name Luminal.

felony
A serious crime, punishable by a prison sentence.

flashback
Slang name for the reappearance of LSD-like effects long after the last dose of LSD was taken.

generic name
A common name assigned to a drug, usually derived from the chemical name.

gin
An alcoholic beverage made from grain and flavored with juniper berries.

glue-sniffing
The deliberate inhaling of fumes from glue or other products.

glutethimide
Common name for a minor tranquilizer with the trade name Doriden.

goof balls
A slang name for sedatives.

grass
A slang name for marijuana.

H
A slang name for heroin.

hallucination
A state of mind in which one sees, hears, smells, or feels things that are not there.

hallucinogen
A drug that can affect the mind in such a way as to cause hallucinations (also referred to as a hallucinogenic drug).

hangover

A slang term for the temporary illness that usually follows recovery from drunkenness.

hashish

A strong mixture of drugs that come from the Indian hemp plant.

hay

A slang name for marijuana.

hearts

A slang name for Benzedrine or Dexedrine.

heroin

A narcotic drug made from morphine.

heroin addict

A person dependent on heroin.

high

A slang term for the immediate intoxicating effects of a drug.

horse

A slang name for heroin.

idiot pills

A slang name for a barbiturate with the trade name Luminal.

intravenous injection

Injecting a drug directly into a vein.

isopropanol

Rubbing alcohol, a poisonous drug.

I.V.

Abbreviation for an intravenous injection.

jag

A slang name for the initial effects of organic solvent vapors.

joints

A slang name for marijuana cigarettes.

Librium

Trade name for the minor tranquilizer chlordiazepoxide.

lid-poppers

A slang name for stimulant drugs.

LSD (or LSD-25)

Commonly used abbreviation for the chemical *ly*sergic acid *d*iethylamide, a hallucinogenic drug which comes from the ergot fungus.

Luminal

Trade name for the barbiturate phenobarbital.

mainlining

A slang term for intravenous injection.

major tranquilizers

A group of potent non-barbiturate sedatives used in the treatment of certain mental illnesses.

marijuana

A mixture of drugs made from the flowering tops and leaves of the Indian hemp plant.

medicines

Drugs given by doctors for the treatment of disease.

meperidine

A narcotic drug made from simple chemicals with the trade name Demerol.

meprobamate

Common name for a minor tranquilizer with the trade names Miltown and Equanil.

mescaline

A hallucinogenic drug that comes from peyote, derived from a cactus.

metabolism

The body's way of burning up food and turning it into energy.

methadone

A narcotic drug made from simple chemicals with the trade name Dolophine.

methamphetamine

Common name for an amphetamine with the trade names Methedrine and Desoxyn.

methanol

Methyl alcohol, a poisonous drug, which in small quantities can cause blindness and death.

Methedrine

A trade name for methamphetamine.

methprylon

Common name for a minor tranquilizer with the trade name Noludar.

methylphenidate

Common name for a stimulant with the trade name Ritalin.

Miltown

A trade name for the minor tranquilizer meprobamate.

minor tranquilizers
A group of non-barbiturate sedatives.

morphine
A narcotic drug made from opium.

narcotics
A class of pain-killing drugs made from opium; also includes certain manufactured drugs that have opium-like effects.

Nembutal
Trade name for the barbiturate pentobarbital.

Noludar
Trade name for the minor tranquilizer methprylon.

non-barbiturates
A large class of sedatives including the major and minor tranquilizers.

O.D.
Slang term for an overdose of a drug.

opium
A narcotic mixture of drugs from the opium poppy.

opium poppy
A flowering plant.

oranges
A slang name for Dexedrine.

organic solvents
A class of chemical compounds used to dissolve other substances.

paranoid psychosis
A severely disturbed mental state in which a person thinks everyone is against him.

paregoric

A liquid preparation containing small amounts of opium, which is used to treat diarrhea.

peaches

A slang name for Benzedrine.

pentobarbital

Common name for a barbiturate with the trade name Nembutal.

pep pills

A slang name for stimulant drugs.

peyote

A mixture of drugs made from the peyote cactus.

phenmetrazine

Common name for the stimulant with the trade name Preludin.

phenobarbital

Common name for the barbiturate with the trade name Luminal.

physical dependence

The body's need to continue taking a drug.

pinks

A slang name for a barbiturate with the trade name Seconal.

Placidyl

Trade name for the minor tranquilizer ethchlorvinal.

pot

A slang name for marijuana.

pot-head

A slang name for a heavy user of marijuana.

pot party

A slang expression for a party where marijuana is widely used.

Preludin

Trade name for the stimulant phenmetrazine.

psilocybin

A hallucinogenic drug that comes from a certain type of mushroom.

psychological dependence

The mind's need to continue taking a drug.

psychosis (or, psychotic reaction)

A state in which hallucinations and a loss of touch with reality commonly occur. It is sometimes the result of drug abuse, sometimes the result of certain severe types of mental illness.

pusher

Slang name for a person who sells drugs illegally.

rainbows

A slang name for a combination of barbiturates with the trade name Tuinal.

red birds, red devils, reds

Slang names for a barbiturate with the trade name Seconal.

reefers

A slang name for marijuana cigarettes.

return trip

A slang name for the reappearance of LSD-like effects long after the last dose of LSD was taken.

Ritalin

Trade name for the stimulant methylphenidate.

rum

An alcoholic beverage made from molasses.

rush

Slang term for the immediate sensation following an intravenous injection of narcotic or stimulant.

rye

An alcoholic beverage made from rye grain.

Scotch

An alcoholic beverage made in Scotland, usually from barley.

secobarbital

Common name for the barbiturate Seconal.

Seconal

Trade name for secobarbital.

sedate

To calm, relax, or relieve nervousness or tension.

sedatives

A group of drugs that slow down the activity of the brain and other parts of the body.

Seggys

A slang name for Seconal.

shooting

A slang term for injecting a drug directly into a vein.

smack

A slang name for heroin.

sobering up

The process of recovering from drunkenness.

speed

A slang name for Methedrine; also for stimulant drugs in general.

sticks

A slang name for marijuana cigarettes.

stimulants

Drugs that increase the activity of the brain and other parts of the nervous system.

STP

Commonly used abbreviation for one of the hallucinogenic drugs made from simple chemicals.

strung out

A slang phrase meaning addicted, usually to narcotics.

tolerance

Condition in which the body has become used to a drug, so that more of the drug is needed to produce the same effect.

toluene

An organic solvent.

Tooies

A slang name for a combination of barbiturates with the trade name Tuinal.

trade name

A name given to a brand of drug that is manufactured by a particular company.

trip

A slang name for the effects of LSD.

Tuinal

Trade name for a combination of amobarbital and secobarbital.

uppers, ups
Slang names for stimulant drugs.

Valium
Trade name for the minor tranquilizer diazepam.

vodka
An alcoholic beverage usually made from rye.

wake-ups
Slang name for stimulant drugs.

weed
A slang name for marijuana.

wine
An alcoholic beverage made from grapes or other fruit.

withdrawal illness
The sickness that results when a person who is physically dependent on a drug suddenly stops taking it.

xanthines
A class of weak stimulants found in coffee, tea, cocoa, and colas—for example, caffeine.

yellow jackets
Slang name for a barbiturate with the trade name Nembutal.

Index

Amytal, 60, 100
aspirin, 6

B-20's, 69, 100
bad trip, 53–54, 100
barbs, 59, 100 (see also SEDATIVES)
barbiturates, 58–59, 60, 100
beer, 79, 80, 100
bennies, 69, 100
Benzedrine, 68, 69, 100
benzene, 91, 101
bhang, 33, 101
Biphetamine, 69, 101
black beauty, 69, 101
blue heaven, 60, 101
bourbon, 79, 101
brandy, 79, 101

cartwheels, 69, 101
calories in alcohol, 80, 101
chlordiazepoxide, 60, 101
Christmas trees, 60, 101
chromosomes, 56, 102
cleaning fluid, 91
coasting, 20, 102
cocaine, 67–68, 102
codeine, 16, 17, 102
co-pilots, 69, 102
cough medicine, 17, 81
crystals, 69, 102
cutting, 25, 27, 53, 102

d-amphetamine, 69, 102
d,l-amphetamine, 69, 102

delirium, 64, 88, 102
delirium tremens, 88, 102
Demerol, 17, 103
depressants, 77, 81–82, 103 (see also SEDATIVES)
Desoxyn, 69, 103
DET, 57, 103
Dexedrine, 68, 69, 103
dexes, 69, 103
diazepam, 60, 103
DMT, 57, 103
DOET, 57, 103
Dolophine, 17, 103
DOM, 57, 103
Doriden, 60, 104
downers, downs, 59, 104 (see also SEDATIVES)
drug, 5–6, 104 (see also specific drug names)
    abuse, 9, 104
    and the law, 14–15, 28–29, 43, 56, 89
    reasons for, 10–12, 13, 93–94, 96–98
    treatment, 14
    effect, 6, 8, 104
    medicine, 6, 107
    antibiotic, 6
    pain-killers, 6, 16–17
    naming, 8–9
    common name, 8
    generic name, 8, 9, 105
    trade name, 8–9, 113
    ways of taking, 8
drug addict, 23, 25, 41, 104

Picture Credits